This journal belongs to

....

A Mother's Heritage
© 2009 Ellie Claire Gift & Paper Corp.
www.ellieclaire.com

Compiled by Barbara Farmer
Designed by Lisa and Jeff Franke for Ellie Claire, Minneapolis, MN

ISBN 978-1-934770-78-8

Printed in China

A MOTHER'S
Heritage

A Loving Keepsake
FOR YOUR CHILDREN

your life, your love, your words

Ellie Claire

gift & paper expressions

...inspired by life

Table of Contents

Introduction

A Mother's Heritage

A Loving Keepsake for Your Children

Each year the seasons change; it is a tradition of creation so that life can progress and move forward. Our lives, too, have seasons where we grow and change, blossom and mature. A family holds generations of seasons, flowing in and out of youth and age, memories and dreams.

As a mother, you live your own life, but you are also given the special privilege of bearing new life—nurturing, guiding, and releasing. This connection is intense and thrilling.

Through the seasonal events of a year, reflect on the memories, the milestones, and the emotions that your heart holds dear for your children and your family in the pages of *A Mother's Heritage*. It is your life written out in your words to convey your love to those who mean the most.

My Self Portrait

My Full Given Name: ....

The Meaning of My Name: ....

Nickname(s): ....

Date and Place of Birth: ....

Sibling Names and Birthdays: ....

....

....

Date and Place of Marriage: ....

Husband's Full Given Name: ....

Names and Birthdays of My Children: ....

....

....

....

My Spiritual Birthday: ....

My Life Verse: ....

....

....

....

....

My Family Tree

Father

    Grandfather

        Great-Grandfather

        Great-Grandmother

    Grandmother

        Great-Grandfather

        Great-Grandmother

Mother

    Grandfather

        Great-Grandfather

        Great-Grandmother

    Grandmother

        Great-Grandfather

        Great-Grandmother

Spring

*Train up a child in the way he should go,
and when he is old he will not depart from it.*

Proverbs 22:6 NKJV

The Days of My Youth

....

....

....

....

....

When I grew up I always wanted to be . . . .

....

....

....

....

....

....

....

I knew I had the talent to . . .
My parents encouraged me to . . .

There is nothing higher and stronger and more useful for life . . . than some good memory, especially a memory connected . . . with home.

Fyodor Dostoyevsky

The Days of My Youth

....

....

....

....

....

My bedroom looked like . . . .
I shared it with . . .

....

....

....

....

....

....

....

....

....

May the favor of the Lord our God rest upon us; establish the work of our hands for us—yes, establish the work of our hands.

Psalm 90:17 NIV

The Days of My Youth

....

....

....

....

....

My father worked at . . . .

....

....

....

....

....

....

....

....

As a mother, my job is to take care of what is possible and trust God with the impossible.

Ruth Bell Graham

The Days of My Youth

....

....

....

....

....

My Mother spent her day . . . .

....

....

....

....

....

....

....

....

She had many jobs like . . .

Consider it pure joy, my brothers, whenever you face trials of many kinds, because you know that the testing of your faith develops perseverance. Perseverance must finish its work so that you may be mature and complete, not lacking anything.

James 1:2-4 NIV

The Days of My Youth

....

....

....

....

....

Some of the happiest times were . . . .

....

....

....

....

....

....

....

....

....

The difficult times taught me . . .

What will your children remember? We can change the world inside our own houses. Take the gift of this moment and make something beautiful of it. Few worthwhile experiences just happen; memories are made on purpose.

Gloria Gaither

The Days of My Youth

....
....
....
....
....

My favorite pastime as a child was . . . .

....
....
....
....
....
....
....
....

I always wanted to play with my friend . . .

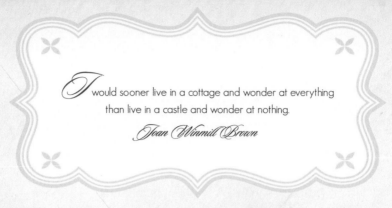

I would sooner live in a cottage and wonder at everything than live in a castle and wonder at nothing.

Joan Winmill Brown

The Days of My Youth

....

....

....

....

....

The most fun thing about our neighborhood was . . . .

....

....

....

....

....

....

....

....

We lived just down the street from . . .

Think back on those early days when you first learned about Christ. Remember how you remained faithful . . . Remember the great reward it brings you!

Hebrews 10:32, 35 NLT

Easter—A Spiritual Awakening

....
....
....
....
....

I first learned about Jesus when I was . . . .
....
....
....
....
....
....
....
....
....

The person who introduced me to Christ was . . .

There is always one moment in childhood when the door opens and lets the future in.

Graham Greene

Easter—A Spiritual Awakening

....
....
....
....
....

I first went to Sunday School . . . .

....
....
....
....
....
....
....
....

On Sundays, we always . . .

*Fix these words of mine in your hearts and minds;
tie them as symbols on your hands and bind them on your foreheads.
Teach them to your children.*

Deuteronomy 11:18-19 NIV

Easter—A Spiritual Awakening

....

....

....

....

....

My first Bible was given to me by . . . .

....

....

....

....

....

....

....

....

My favorite Bible stories were/are . . .

....

....

....

....

....

....

....

....

....

....

....

....

....

....

....

....

....

....

he serene beauty of a holy life is the most powerful influence in the world next to the power of God.

Blaise Pascal

Easter—A Spiritual Awakening

....

....

....

....

he people who influence me now in my Christian walk are . . . .

....

....

....

....

....

....

....

....

What I cherish most about my faith . . .

Mother's Day—Past, Present, Future

....

....

....

....

....

What my mother means to me . . . .

....

....

....

....

....

....

....

....

What it means for me to be a mother . . .

33

I bow in prayer before the Father from whom every family in heaven and on earth gets its true name. I ask the Father in His great glory to give you the power to be strong inwardly through His Spirit.

Ephesians 3:14-16 NCV

Mother's Day—Past, Present, Future

....
....
....
....
....

Motherhood has changed so much . . . .
....
....
....
....
....
....
....
....
....

*W*hen I was picking out names . . .

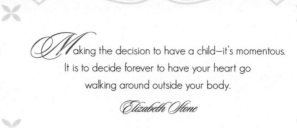

*Making the decision to have a child—it's momentous.
It is to decide forever to have your heart go
walking around outside your body.*

Elizabeth Stone

Mother's Day—Past, Present, Future

....

....

....

....

....

Experiencing motherhood for the first time . . . .

....

....

....

....

....

....

....

....

When I was pregnant I'll never forget . . .

I have not stopped thanking God for you.
I pray for you constantly, asking God, the glorious Father
of our Lord Jesus Christ, to give you spiritual wisdom and insight
so that you might grow in your knowledge of God.

Ephesians 1:16-17 NLT

Mother's Day—Past, Present, Future

*H*olding my child for the first time I felt . . .

The prayers I have for my children . . .

39

God is the Father who is full of mercy and all comfort. He comforts us every time we have trouble, so when others have trouble, we can comfort them with the same comfort God gives us.

2 Corinthians 1:3-4 NCV

Memorial Day

....
....
....
....
....

When I lost someone very close to me . . . .

....
....
....
....
....
....
....
....

What I've learned about making the most of what we're given . . .

Children who mature into stable young adults almost always have had a caring adult figure who has been a positive model in their life.

Doug Fields

Memorial Day

$\mathcal{A}$ loved one who inspired me . . .

My heroes are . . .

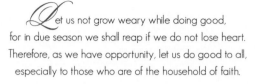

*et us not grow weary while doing good,
for in due season we shall reap if we do not lose heart.
Therefore, as we have opportunity, let us do good to all,
especially to those who are of the household of faith.*

Galatians 6:9-10 NKJV

Memorial Day

The causes that I would fight for are . . .

The people I knew who served in the military . . .

Summer

*Lord, You are our Father.
We are like clay, and You are the potter;
Your hands made us all.
Isaiah 64:8 NCV*

Father's Day

_My_ father or father-figure was . . .

In his own way, he showed me my Heavenly Father . . .

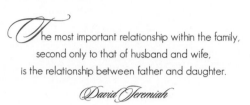

he most important relationship within the family,
second only to that of husband and wife,
is the relationship between father and daughter.

David Jeremiah

Father's Day

....

....

....

....

....

*D*addy's view of his little girl . . . .

....

....

....

....

....

....

....

....

When I started dating . . .

*Pay close attention, friend, to what your father tells you;
never forget what you learned at your mother's knee. Wear their
counsel like flowers in your hair, like rings on your fingers.*

Proverbs 1:8-9 THE MESSAGE

Father's Day

....

....

....

....

....

The time I spent with my dad was . . . .

....

....

....

....

....

....

....

....

*W*hen Dad came home from work, he would always . . .

*The most important thing a father can do for his children
is to love their mother.*

Theodore M. Hesburgh

Father's Day

....
....
....
....
....

The relationship between my mother and father was. . . ..

....
....
....
....
....
....
....
....
....

*S*ome of my father's traits I looked for in a husband . . .

....

....

....

....

....

....

....

....

....

....

....

....

....

....

....

....

....

....

....

....

ood friend, follow your father's good advice; don't wander off from your mother's teachings.... Wherever you walk, they'll guide you; whenever you rest, they'll guard you; when you wake up, they'll tell you what's next.

Proverbs 6:20-22 THE MESSAGE

Father's Day

....

....

....

....

....

ow, as a grownup, I look at my father and see . . . .

....

....

....

....

....

....

....

He really taught me the importance of . . .

....
....
....
....
....
....
....
....
....
....
....
....
....
....

*N*ever drive faster than your guardian angel can fly.

Independence Day

....

....

....

....

....

*M*y first time driving alone . . . .

....

....

....

....

....

....

....

....

....

You should have seen my first car . . .

59

The Lord says, "I will make you wise and show you where to go. I will guide you and watch over you."

Psalm 32:8 NCV

Independence Day

....

....

....

....

My first trip by plane / train / boat . . . .

....

....

....

....

....

....

....

....

My travel experience reaches as far as . . .

If you think there are no new frontiers,
watch a boy ring the front doorbell on his first date.
Olin Miller

Independence Day

....

....

....

....

....

I had my first date when I was . . . .

....

....

....

....

....

....

....

....

We went to the . . .

*Think only about the things in heaven, not the things on earth . . .
your new life is kept with Christ in God.*

Colossians 3:2-3 NCV

Independence Day

....

....

....

....

....

The main influence I had while developing my worldview was . . . .

....

....

....

....

....

....

....

....

I felt like I needed to defend my beliefs when . . .

*Open your eyes, your ears, your mind, your heart,
your spirit and you'll find adventure everywhere . . . .
Think of whatever you are doing as an adventure
and watch your life change for the better.*

Wilferd A. Peterson

Independence Day

....

....

....

....

....

I'll never forget the first time I was out on my own . . . .

....

....

....

....

....

....

....

....

With God's power working in us, God can do much, much more than anything we can ask or imagine.

Ephesians 3:20 NCV

Independence Day

....
....
....
....
....

My goals and dreams were/are . . . .

....
....
....
....
....
....
....

Some of the dreams and goals I have fulfilled . . .

For whatever life holds for you and your family in the coming days, weave the unfailing fabric of God's Word through your heart and mind. It will hold strong, even if the rest of life unravels.

Gigi Graham Tchividjian

Independence Day

_____

_____

_____

_____

_____

The most difficult choice I ever had to make was . . . _____

_____

_____

_____

_____

_____

_____

_____

_____

_____

If given the chance to do it over, I would . . .

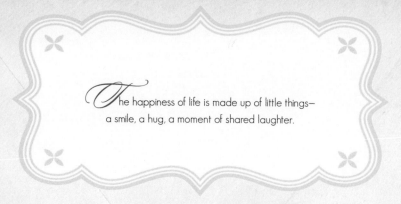

*The happiness of life is made up of little things—
a smile, a hug, a moment of shared laughter.*

"The Dog Days of Summer"

....

....

....

....

....

Our family vacations were famous for . . . .

....

....

....

....

....

....

....

....

There was always summer camp or group activities...

*Children do not grow up gradually.
They move forward in spurts
like the hands of clocks in railway stations.*

Cyril Connolly

"The Dog Days of Summer"

The organization(s) I participated in . . .

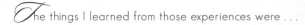

The things I learned from those experiences were . . .

*Surprise us with love at daybreak;
then we'll skip and dance all the day long.*

Psalm 90:14 THE MESSAGE

"The Dog Days of Summer"

....

....

....

....

....

When I played dress up, I liked to be . . . .

....

....

....

....

....

....

....

....

My special place to play was . . .

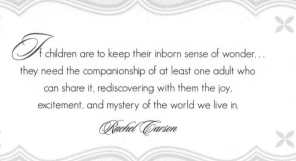

If children are to keep their inborn sense of wonder...
they need the companionship of at least one adult who
can share it, rediscovering with them the joy,
excitement, and mystery of the world we live in.

Rachel Carson

"The Dog Days of Summer"

....
....
....
....

My first pet was a . . . .

....
....
....
....
....
....
....
....

"The Dog Days of Summer"

My favorite author/book when I was a child . . . When I was a teenage . . .

Now I love to read . . .

....

....

....

....

....

....

....

....

....

....

....

....

....

....

....

*A*re you tired? Worn out?... Come to me.
Get away with me and you'll recover your life.
I'll show you how to take a real rest.

Matthew 11:28 THE MESSAGE

"The Dog Days of Summer"

....
....
....
....
....

*M*y favorite way to relax is . . . .
....
....
....
....
....
....
....
....
....

I first learned to swim . . . ride a bike . . . ski . . . roller skate . . .

Autumn

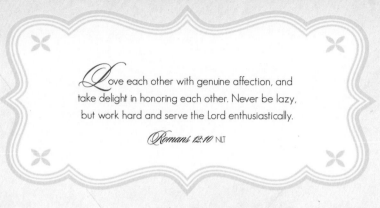

Love each other with genuine affection, and take delight in honoring each other. Never be lazy, but work hard and serve the Lord enthusiastically.

Romans 12:10 NLT

Labor Day

Some of my hobbies were/are . . .

loved to help out with . . .

All work, from the simplest chore to the most challenging and complex undertaking, is a wonder and a miracle. It is a gift and a blessing that God has given us . . . . To work is to do something essential to our humanness.

Ben Patterson

Labor Day

....

....

....

....

The chores I had to do every day/week were . . . .

....

....

....

....

....

....

....

My allowance was based on . . .

89

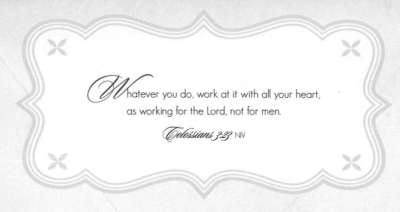

*Whatever you do, work at it with all your heart,
as working for the Lord, not for men.*

Colossians 3:23 NIV

Labor Day

....
....
....
....

....

My first real job was working for . . . .
....
....
....
....
....
....
....
....

The most special thing I bought with my earnings was . . .

Slow down awhile! Push aside the press of the immediate. Take time today, if only for a moment, to lovingly encourage each one in your family.

Gary Smalley and John Trent

Labor Day

....

....

....

....

....

For weekend fun, my family/friends and I would . . . .

....

....

....

....

....

....

....

....

....

ll never forget the time we . . .

> My child, eat honey, for it is good, and the honeycomb
> is sweet to the taste. In the same way, wisdom is sweet
> to your soul. If you find it, you will have a bright future,
> and your hopes will not be cut short.
>
> *Proverbs 24:13-14* NLT

School Days

In elementary school my favorite teacher was . . .

The teacher that impressed me the most in high school was . . .

....

....

....

....

....

....

....

....

....

....

....

....

....

....

....

....

In my day, we couldn't afford shoes, so we went barefoot. In the winter we had to wrap our feet with barbed wire for traction.

Bill Flavin

School Days

....

....

....

....

....

In order to get to school I had to . . . .

....

....

....

....

....

....

....

$\mathcal{L}$unch time consisted of . . .

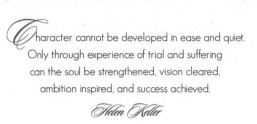

Character cannot be developed in ease and quiet. Only through experience of trial and suffering can the soul be strengthened, vision cleared, ambition inspired, and success achieved.

Helen Keller

School Days

....

....

....

....

....

A learning experiences I'll never forget . . . .

....

....

....

....

....

....

....

....

Extra-curricular activities I participated in . . .

*G*od's various gifts are handed out everywhere;
but they all originate in God's Spirit . . . .
Each person is given something to do that shows who God is:
Everyone gets in on it, everyone benefits.

1 Corinthians 12:4, 7 THE MESSAGE

School Days

I always excelled at . . .

My least favorite subject was . . .

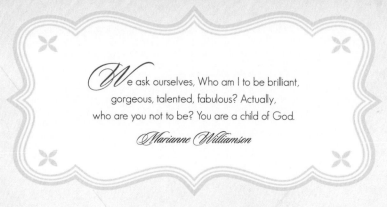

We ask ourselves, Who am I to be brilliant,
gorgeous, talented, fabulous? Actually,
who are you not to be? You are a child of God.

Marianne Williamson

School Days

The style-of-the-day was to wear . . .

My hair-do looked like . . .

*I'm asking God for one thing, only one thing:
To live with Him n His house my whole life long.
I'll contemplate His beauty; I'll study at His feet.*

Psalm 27:4 THE MESSAGE

School Days

I went to college/trade school at . . .

My major field of study was . . .
Degrees and honors I earned . . .

Of all best things upon the earth,
I hold that a faithful friend is the best.

Edward G. Bulwer-Lytton

School Days

My best friend was . . .

I was known by my friends for . . .

*B*ut from everlasting to everlasting
the Lord's love is with those who fear Him,
and His righteousness with their children's children.

Psalm 103:17 NIV

Grandparent's Day

*L*et me tell you about my grandparents . . .

Going to Grandma and Grandpa's house was . . .

Grandmas don't just say "that's nice"—they reel back and roll their eyes and throw up their hands and smile. You get your money's worth out of grandmas.

Grandparent's Day

....

....

....

....

....

My best memory of Grandma is . . . .

....

....

....

....

....

....

....

....

Grandma would always treat us to . . .

My grandfather was a wonderful role model.
Through him I got to know the gentle side of men.
Sarah Long

Grandparent's Day

Grandpa's favorite thing to say was . . .

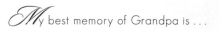

My best memory of Grandpa is . . .

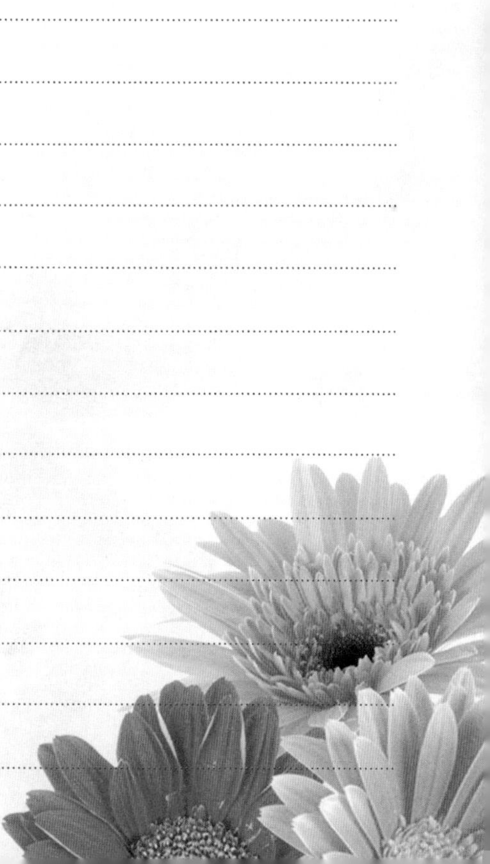

What will your children remember?
There is something in every season, in every day,
to celebrate with thanksgiving.
Gloria Gaither

Thanksgiving

....

....

....

....

....

The most memorable Thanksgiving I ever had was . . . .

....

....

....

....

....

....

....

....

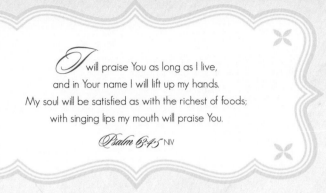

I will praise You as long as I live,
and in Your name I will lift up my hands.
My soul will be satisfied as with the richest of foods;
with singing lips my mouth will praise You.

Psalm 63:4-5 NIV

Thanksgiving

*T*he main dishes were always . . .

The first time I contributed to the meal I made . . .

When you look at your life,
the greatest happinesses are family happinesses.

Joyce Brothers

Thanksgiving

....
....
....
....
....

Who showed up for the big meal . . . .

....
....
....
....
....
....
....
....

*A*fter we ate, we would always . . .

*Enter into His gates with thanksgiving, and into His courts
with praise. Be thankful to Him, and bless His name.
For the Lord is good; His mercy is everlasting,
And His truth endures to all generations.*

Psalm 100:4-5 NKJV

Thanksgiving

....

....

....

....

....

When I was growing up I was thankful for . . . .

....

....

....

....

....

....

....

....

*N*ow that I'm a grownup I'm thankful for . . .

Winter

Celebrate God all day, every day. I mean, revel in Him! Make it as clear as you can to all you meet that you're on their side . . . . Help them see that the Master is about to arrive.

Philippians 4:4-5 THE MESSAGE

Christmas

At our house we started celebrating Christmas . . .

My favorite way to get into the Christmas spirit was to . . .

Cleaning your house while your kids are still growing
Is like shoveling the walk before it stops snowing.

Phyllis Diller

Christmas

....
....
....
....
....

Oh, the weather outside was usually . . . .

....
....
....
....
....
....
....
....
....

I dreamed of a White Christmas, and . . .

I pray that from His glorious, unlimited resources He will empower you with inner strength through His Spirit. Then Christ will make His home in your hearts as you trust in Him. Your roots will grow down into God's love and keep you strong.

Ephesians 3:16-17 NLT

Christmas

....
....
....
....

....

*W*hen we stayed home for Christmas . . . .

....
....
....
....
....
....
....
....

Trips to Grandmother's house or other relatives were . . .

*L*ife holds no sweeter thing than this—
To teach little children the tale most loved on earth
And watch the wonder deepen in their eyes
The while you tell them of the Christ Child's birth.

Adelaide Love

Christmas

*W*hen there was a Christmas program I would . . .

Some of my favorite carols were . . .

131

*Joseph also went up from Galilee, . . . to the city of David,
which is called Bethlehem, . . . to be registered with Mary,
his betrothed wife, who was with child . . . .
And she brought forth her firstborn Son. . .and laid Him in a manger.*

Luke 2:4-5, 7 NKJV

Christmas

....

....

....

....

....

My favorite Christmas dish has always been . . . .

....

....

....

....

....

....

....

....

*O*ur most cherished family tradition was . . .

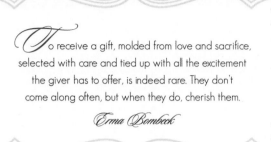

*To receive a gift, molded from love and sacrifice,
selected with care and tied up with all the excitement
the giver has to offer, is indeed rare. They don't
come along often, but when they do, cherish them.*

Erma Bombeck

Christmas

If I could give any gift to any one, I would give . . .

The most unforgettable gift I've ever received was . . .

*Life is like an exciting book,
and every year starts a new chapter.*

New Year's Day

....

....

....

....

....

My favorite New Year's Resolutions was . . . .

....

....

....

....

....

....

....

....

$\mathcal{T}$he best way I've ever celebrated the New Year was . . .

*Your statutes are my heritage forever;
they are the joy of my heart.*

Psalm 119:111 NIV

New Year's Day

....

....

....

....

....

I would like people to describe me as . . . .

....

....

....

....

....

....

....

....

The legacy I want to pass down to my family is . . .

All through the seasons of sowing and reaping,
All through the harvest of song and tears,
Hold us close in Your tender keeping,
O Maker of all New Years!

New Year's Day

When I look back I wish . . .

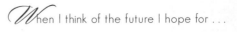
When I think of the future I hope for . . .

So be truly glad. There is wonderful joy ahead, even though you have to endure many trials for a little while.

1 Peter 1:6 NLT

New Year's Day

The hardest year of my life was . . .

The year that turned out the best was . . .

Then we sat on the edge of the earth,
with our feet dangling over the side,
and marveled that we had found each other.

Erik Dillard

Love and the Promise of Spring

....

....

....

....

I met your father when I was . . . .

....

....

....

....

....

....

....

....

The place we met was . . .

145

You've captured my heart, dear friend.
You looked at me, and I fell in love.
One look my way and I was hopelessly in love!

Song of Songs 4:9 THE MESSAGE

Love and the Promise of Spring

....

....

....

....

....

My first impression of him . . . .

....

....

....

....

....

....

....

....

*O*ur first kiss was . . .

147

Our sweetest experiences of affection
are meant to point us to that realm
which is the real and endless home of the heart.

Henry Ward Beecher

Love and the Promise of Spring

I knew he was the one when . . .

When he proposed to me . . .

....
....
....
....
....
....
....
....
....
....
....
....
....
....
....
....
....
....

Love does not consist in gazing at each other
but in looking together in the same direction.

Antoine de Saint-Exupéry

Love and the Promise of Spring

....

....

....

....

....

The day we got married . . . .

....

....

....

....

....

....

....

....

A funny thing happened . . .

There are three things too wonderful for me to understand—no, four! How an eagle glides through the sky. How a serpent crawls upon a rock. How a ship finds its way across the heaving ocean. The growth of love between a man and a girl.

Proverbs 30:18-19 TLB

Love and the Promise of Spring

....

....

....

....

....

We took our honeymoon trip to . . . .

....

....

....

....

....

....

....

....

*O*ur first home was . . .

153

Love grows from our capacity to give what is deepest within ourselves and also receive what is the deepest within another person. The heart becomes an ocean strong and deep, launching all on its tide.

Love and the Promise of Spring

How our love has changed . . .

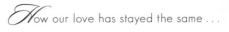
How our love has stayed the same . . .

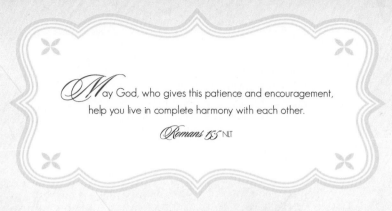

May God, who gives this patience and encouragement, help you live in complete harmony with each other.

Romans 15:5 NLT

Love and the Promise of Spring

....
....
....
....

The most important marital advice I can give you is . . . .

....
....
....
....
....
....
....
....

I pray for you, my children, and your future spouses . . .

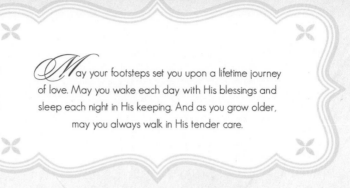

May your footsteps set you upon a lifetime journey of love. May you wake each day with His blessings and sleep each night in His keeping. And as you grow older, may you always walk in His tender care.

Love and the Promise of Spring

....

....

....

....

....

Encouragement and inspiration that has made a difference in my life . . . .

....

....

....

....

....

....

....

I am looking forward most to . . .